Timeless Landscapes

1

国宝・閑谷学校
National Treasure
Shizutani School

millegraph

国宝・閑谷学校
National Treasure
Shizutani School

目次
Table of Content

2 写真：小川重雄
Photographs
Shigeo Ogawa

50 キャプション
Captions

52 図面
Diagrams

60 解説「時を超える知恵の木箱」
西本真一

68 Commentary
"A Wooden Box Containing the Wisdom of the Ages"
Shin'ichi Nishimoto

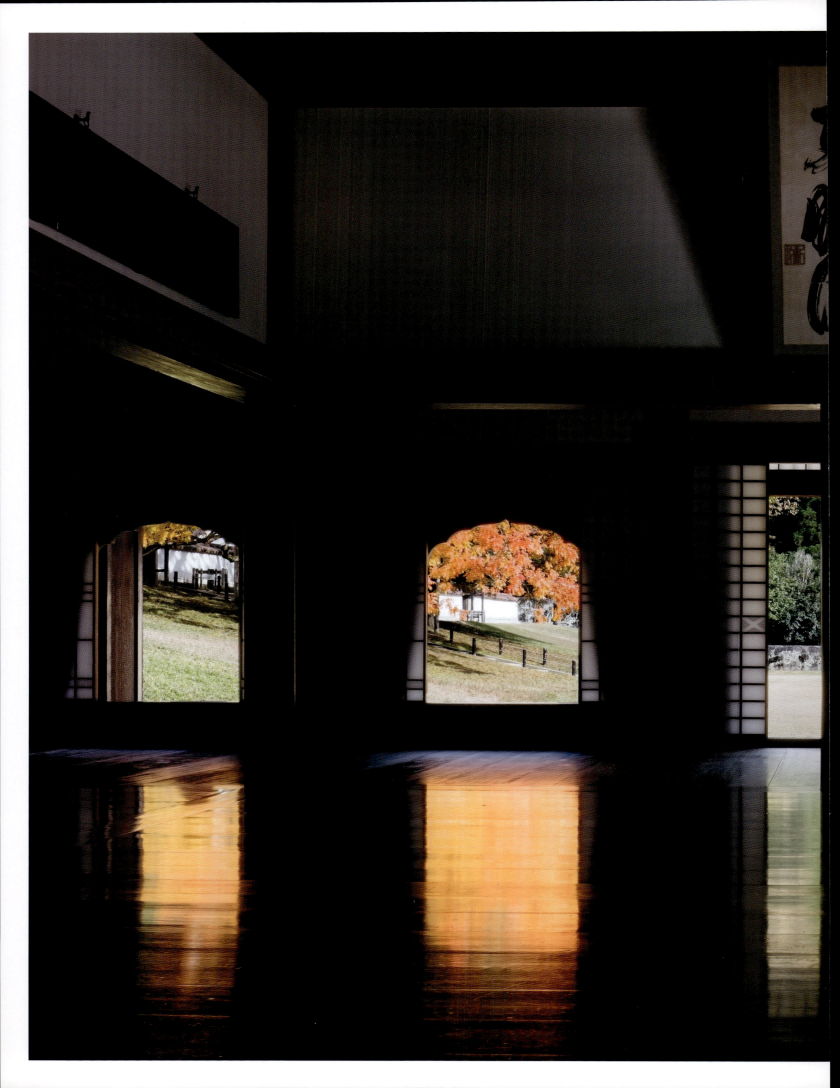

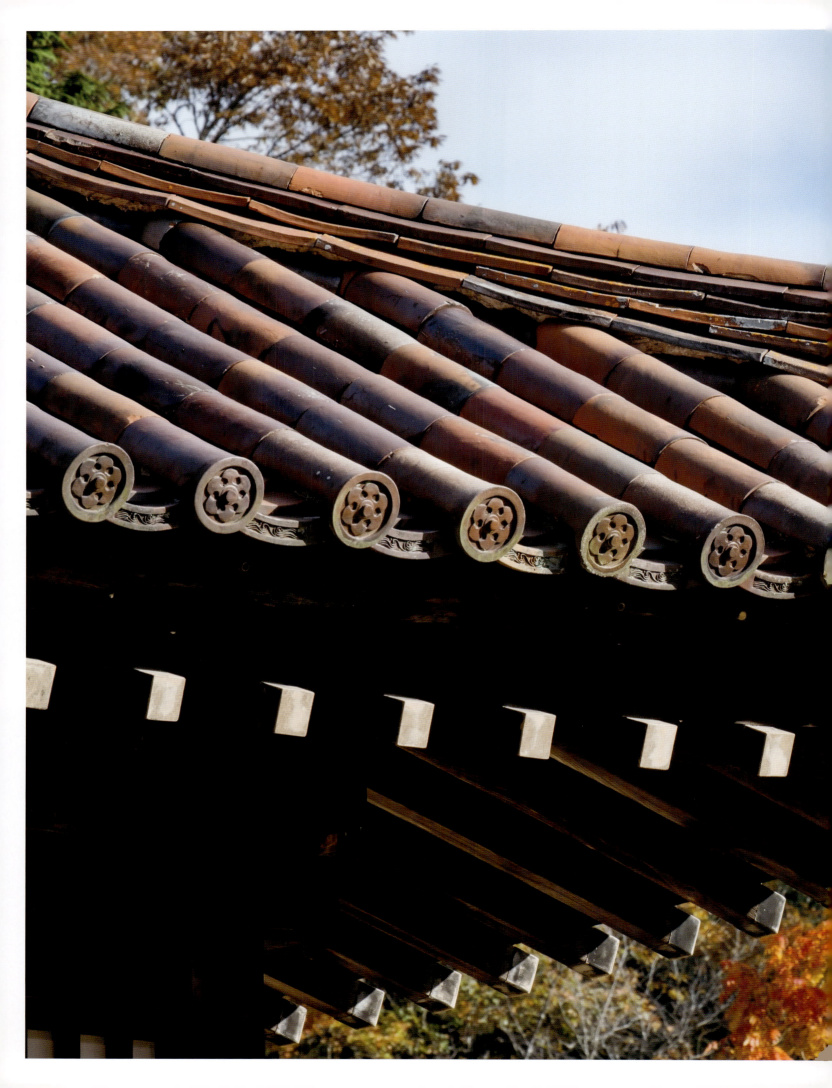

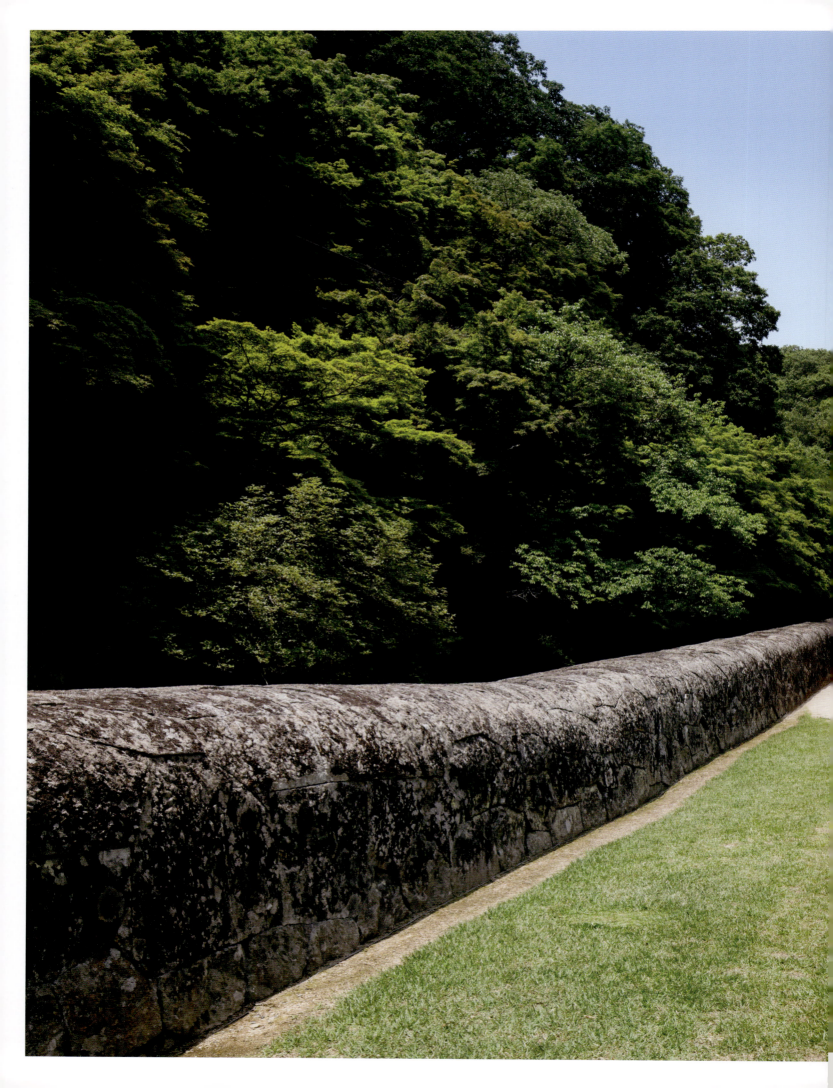

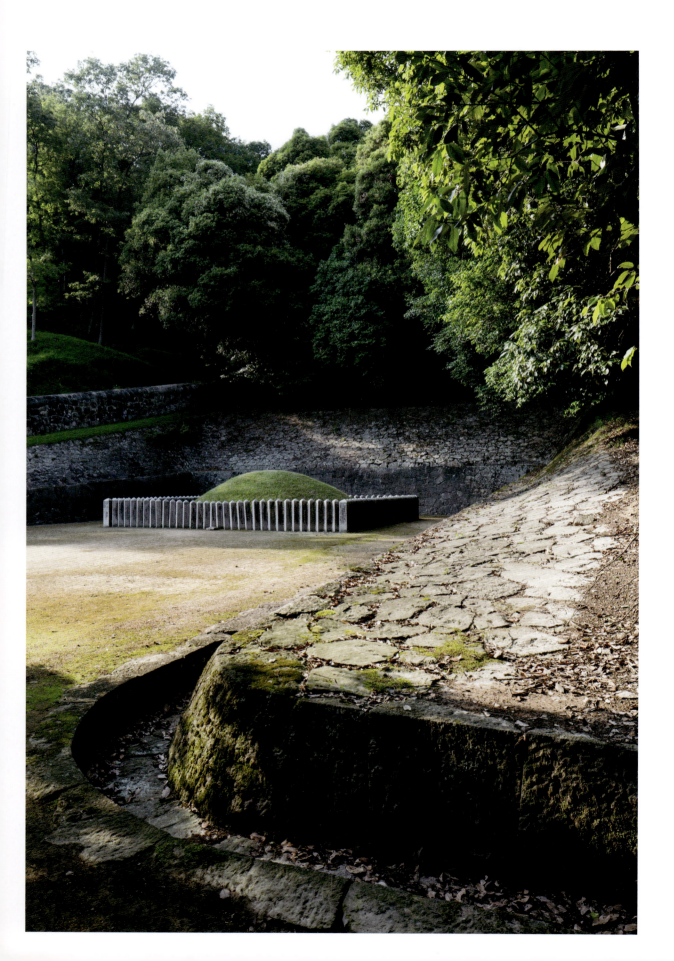

—
キャプション
Captions
—
図面
Diagrams
—
解説
Commentary
—
—
—

キャプション
Captions

図面
Diagrams

解説
Commentary

キャプション
Captions

撮影は2016年5月、同11月に行われた。
Photographs in this volume were taken in May and November of 2016.

pp.2-3　南側より見る。ひときわ大きい「講堂」(1701年建造、国宝)は入母屋造、備前焼の本瓦錣葺き。背後に山を抱える。手前の門は「公門」(1701年建造、重要文化財)。「御成門」とも呼ばれる。
Seen from the south. The large lecture hall (1701, National Treasure) has a *shikorobuki* style hip-and-gable roof (in which the hipped and gabled sections are discontinuous) covered with *honkawara* tiles made of Bizen earthenware. There are hills behind the building. The gate in the foreground, known as the *kōmon* or *onarimon* (1701, Important Cultural Property), was the official gate used during visits by the lord.

pp.6-7　講堂、東立面。左に「小斎」(1677年建造、重要文化財)。屋根は柿葺き。
East face of the lecture hall. The roof of the small study (1677, Important Cultural Property) at left is covered with thin wooden shingles.

pp.8-9　東立面。角柱の上に載る舟肘木が桁を支える。花頭窓の障子を開放。
East face. Boat-shaped bracket arms atop the square pillars support the purlins. Here the shoji panels in the bell-shaped windows are open.

pp.10-11　講堂の縁。内部と外部の中間領域。
Lecture hall veranda, an intermediate zone between interior and exterior.

p.13　欅の円柱。
A round pillar of zelkova wood.

pp.14-17　講堂内、身舎より東側を見る。拭き漆の床に、光や外の景色が映り込む。中央の「克明徳」の書は、備前岡山藩五代藩主・池田治政による。
Lecture hall interior, looking from the core to the east side. The wiped-lacquer finish of the floor reflects the light and the outside scenery. The calligraphy at the center is the work of Ikeda Harumasa, fifth lord of the Okayama domain.

pp.18-19　中央の身舎は梁間2間・桁行3間、計10本の円柱が囲う。その外側に庇、さらにその外側を縁が取り囲んでいる。北側には山裾が迫る。
The central core is three bays wide, two bays deep, and bounded by ten round pillars. This is surrounded by a peripheral zone, which is further surrounded by the veranda. The hills encroach from the north.

p.21　花頭窓より内部を見る。
Interior seen through a bell-shaped window.

pp.22-23　講堂はいま現在も学習の場として使用されている(要予約)。
The lecture hall is still used today as a site for learning. (Reservations required.)

pp.24-25　円柱と花頭窓、床の構成。
Round pillars, bell-shaped windows, and the floor.

pp.26-27　講堂内部は花頭窓からの光を写し取るカメラ・オブスクラとなる。
The lecture hall interior functions like a camera obscura, reflecting the light that comes in through the bell-shaped windows.

p.29　西日を受ける備前焼の瓦屋根。
Bizen ware roof tiles in the light of the setting sun.

pp.30-31　軒の詳細。屋根の下に見える小さな円管は陶製で、万一、瓦の下に水が入ったときの排出口となっている〔p.65の解説参照〕。
Detail of the eaves. The small earthenware pipes visible beneath the roof drain away any water that might manage to get beneath the roof tiles. [See p.72 for details.]

pp.32-33　鳥瞰。特別な許可を得てドローンを使用。各施設の配置はpp.58–59参照。
Bird's-eye view, taken with special permission using a drone. See pages 58–59 for the layout of the buildings.

pp.34-35　かまぼこ型の石塀と講堂の屋根。
The semi-cylindrical stone wall and the roof of the lecture hall.

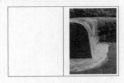
p.37　石塀詳細。
Detail of stone wall.

pp.38-39　斜面を擁する敷地全体を石塀が囲う。石塀の総長は764.9m。
The grounds, which include sloped areas, are entirely enclosed within stone walls with a total length of 764.9 meters.

p.40-41　講堂西側。石塀と「火除け山」、「文庫」(1677年建造、重要文化財)。火除け山は敷地の西端にあった学舎や学房(寄宿舎)で出火した場合、その火が講堂などに及ばないように築かれた。
West side of the lecture hall, showing stone walls, firebreak hill, and library (built 1677, Important Cultural Property). The firebreak hill was built to prevent any outbreak of fire in the school building and dormitory on the western edge of the grounds from spreading to the lecture hall.

pp.42-43　雨に濡れた石塀と紅葉。
Rain-dampened stone walls with autumn foliage.

p.44　池田光政の供養塚「御納所」。
Memorial mound for Ikeda Mitsumasa.

p.45　敷地東側の「椿山」より石塀越しに講堂を見る。
Lecture hall seen beyond the stone wall from Camellia Hill on the east side of the grounds.

pp.46-47　左に「校門」(1701年建造、重要文化財)。中国最古の詩集である「詩経」のなかの詩に因み「鶴鳴門」とも呼ばれる。右に孔子を祀る「聖廟」(1684年建造、重要文化財)と、池田光政を祀る「閑谷神社」(1686年建造、重要文化財)が並ぶ。
The school gate at left (1701, Important Cultural Property) is also called the *kakumeimon* [Gate of the Crying Crane] after a poem in the *Book of Songs*, China's oldest poetry collection. On the right are the Confucian temple (1684, Important Cultural Property) and the Shizutani Shrine (1686, Important Cultural Property), which honors Ikeda Mitsumasa.

図面
Diagrams
—
数字の単位は尺
Figures are expressed in *shaku* [1 *shaku* = 303.03 mm]

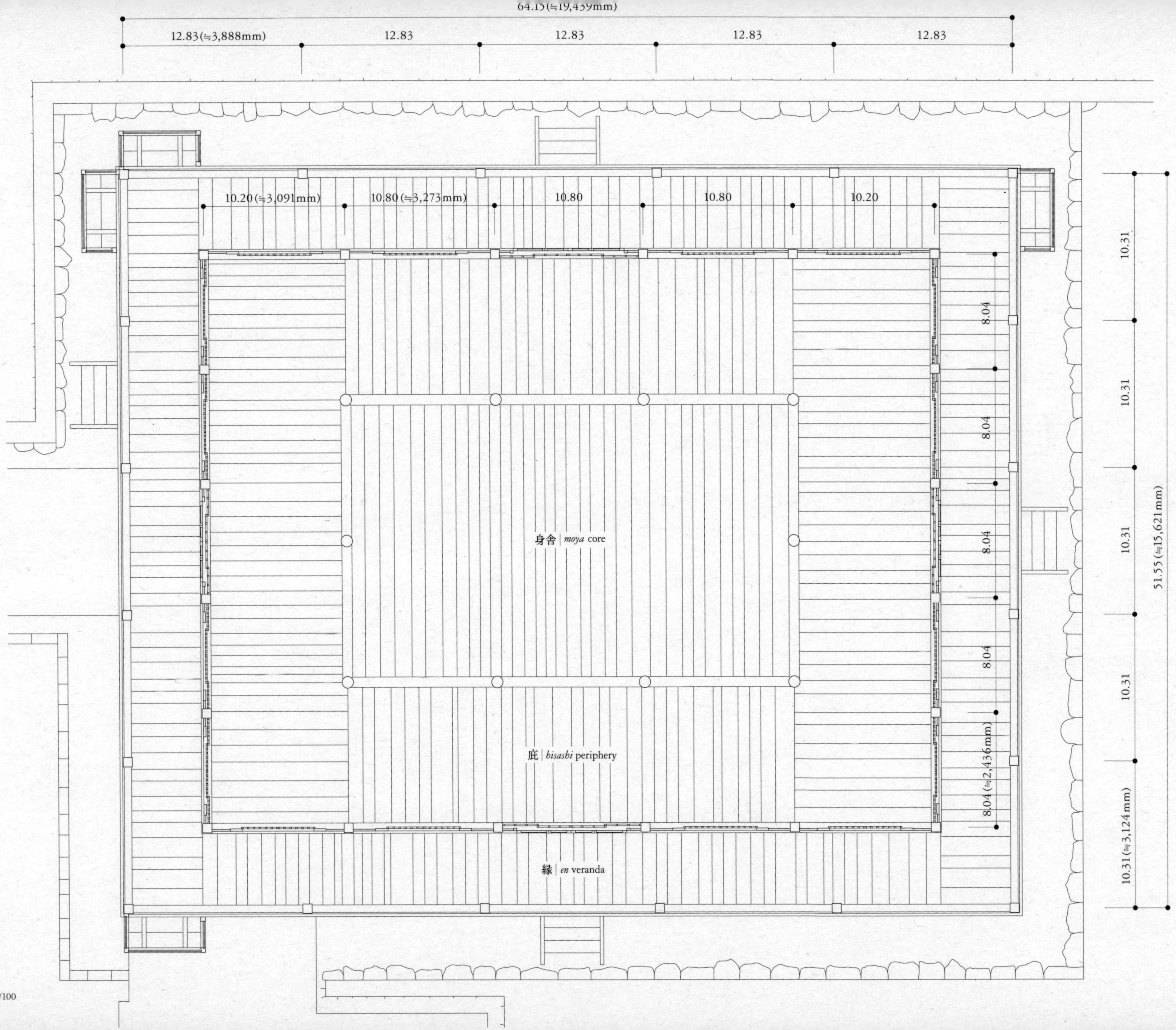

51.55 (≒15,621mm)

10.31 (≒3,124mm) | 10.31 | 10.31 | 10.31

8.04 (≒2,436mm) | 8.04 | 8.04 | 8.04

64.13 (≒19,439mm)

12.83 (≒3,888mm) | 12.83 | 12.83 | 12.83 | 12.83

10.20 (≒3,091mm) | 10.80 (≒3,273mm) | 10.80 | 10.80 | 10.20

身舎 *moya* core

庇 *hisashi* periphery

縁 | *en* veranda

講堂 平面図 1/100
Plan of the Lecture Hall 1/100

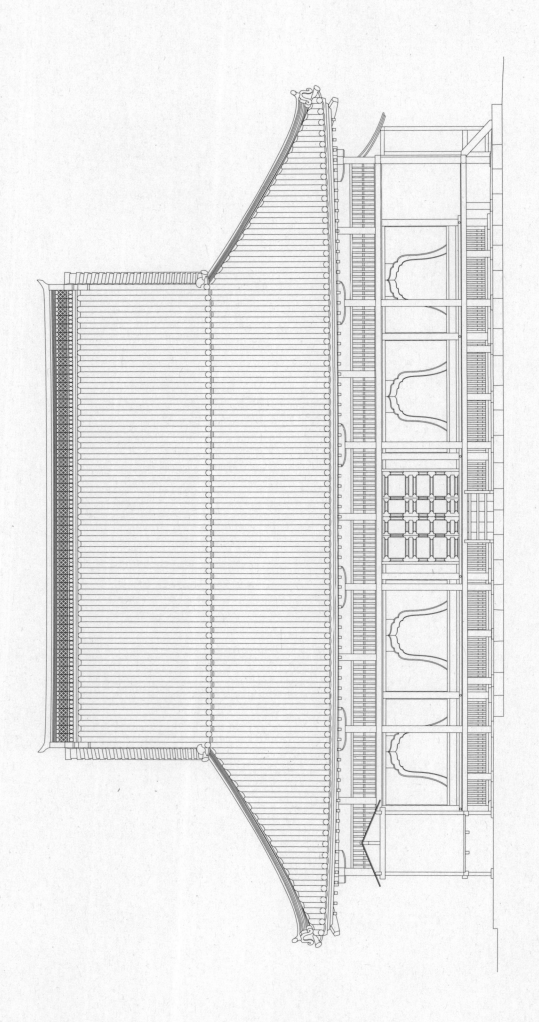

講堂 南立面図 1/100
South Elevation of the Lecture Hall 1/100

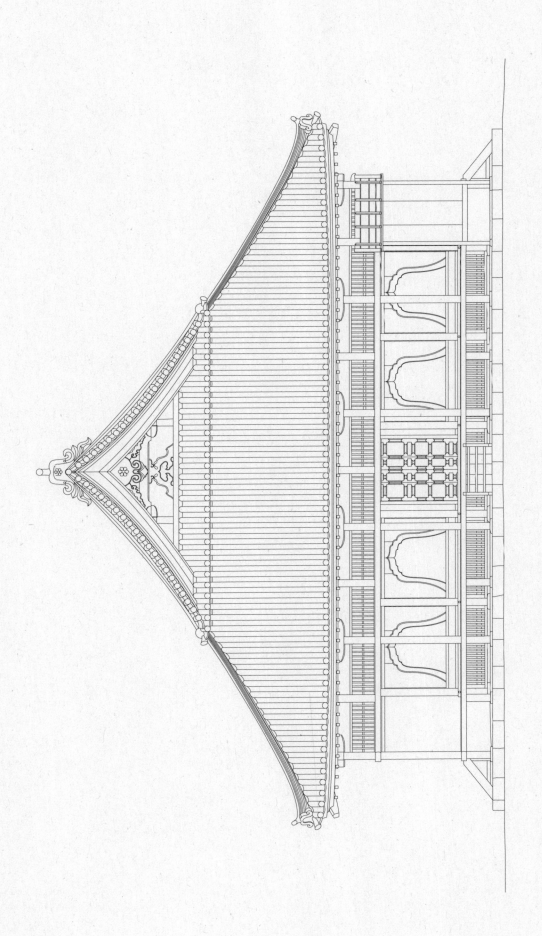

講堂 東立面図 1/100
East Elevation of the Lecture Hall 1/100

講堂 長手断面図 1/100
Longitudinal Section of the Lecture Hall 1/100

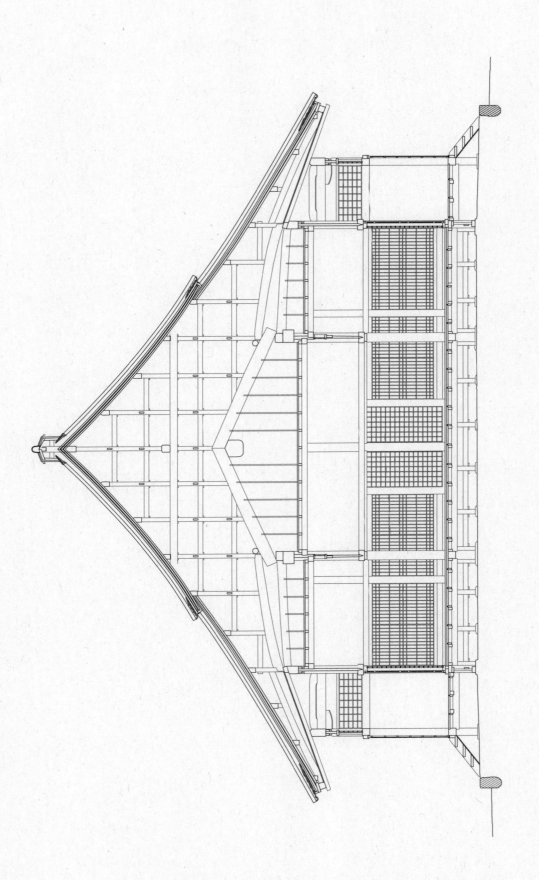

講堂 短手断面図 1/100
Transverse Section of the Lecture Hall 1/100

閑谷学校 配置図 1/1,000
Site Plan of Shizutani School 1/1,000

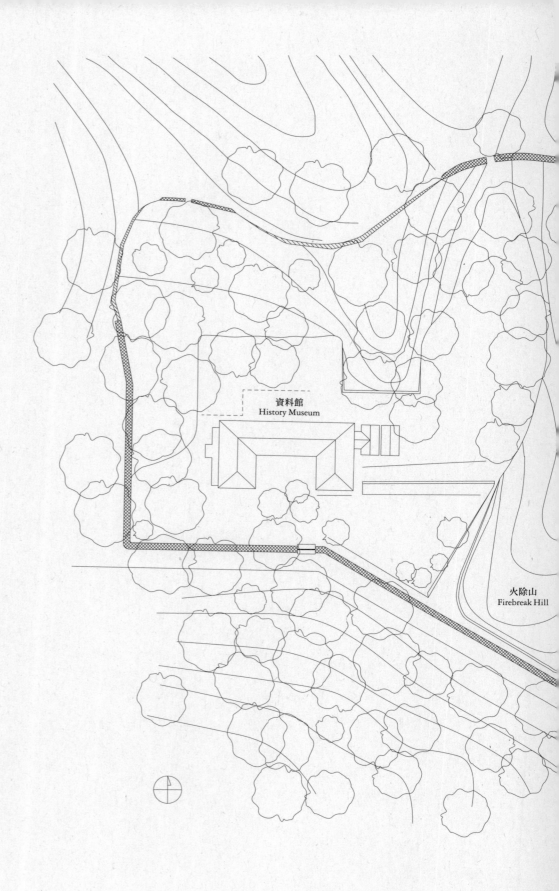

資料館
History Museum

火除山
Firebreak Hill

本配置図は、岡山県教育委員会『特別史蹟並びに国宝及び重要文化財 閑谷黌講堂外四棟保存修理(第一期)工事報告書』(1961)や同『特別史蹟並びに国宝及び重要文化財 閑谷黌聖廟、閑谷神社々殿及び石塀保存修理(第二期)工事報告書』(1962)を元とし、現状に近いかたちに改変して制作。

This diagram is based on the Okayama Prefectural Board of Education's reports on the first and second phases of conservation and repair efforts at Shizutani School, published in 1961 and 1962. Please see the list of references for further details.

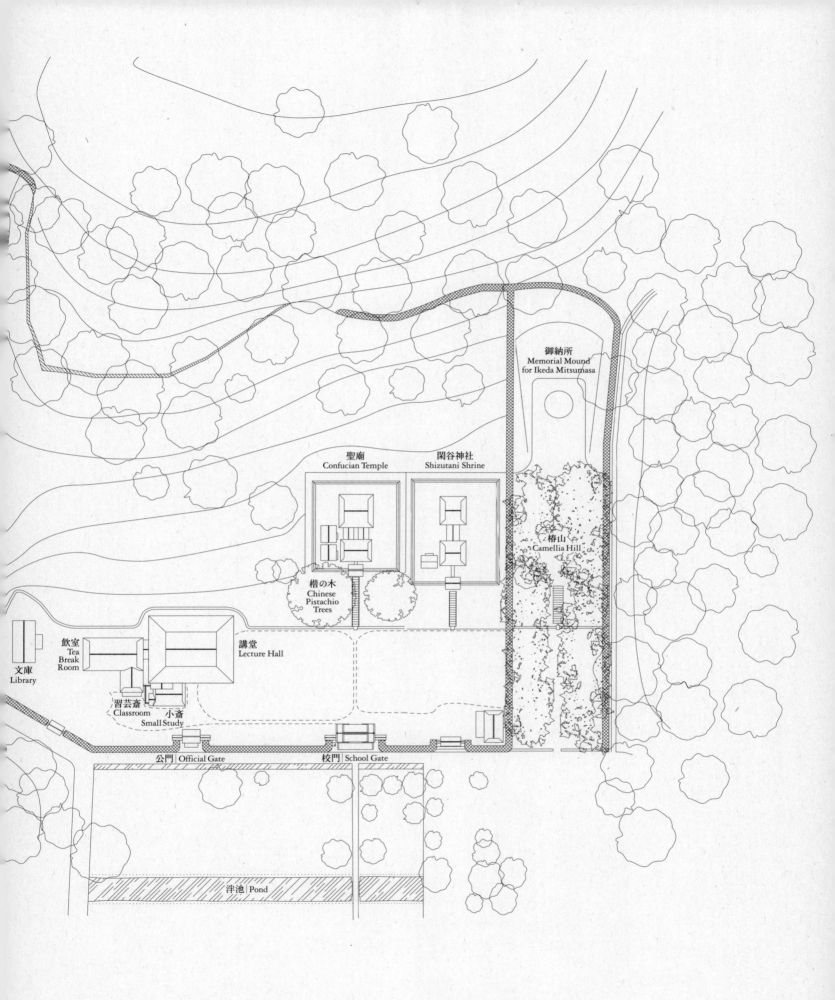

時を超える知恵の木箱｜西本真一

朝方、からからから……、と閑谷学校 講堂（以下、閑谷講堂）の雨戸がすべて開け放たれ、連続する花頭
窓に陽が当たる。

この建物は、日本に現存する最古の学校として名高い。知られている日本の古い学校としては、他に栃木県
の足利学校が挙げられる。その創立は中世にまで遡ると言われており、フランシスコ・ザビエル（1506-52）
による16世紀の書簡にも登場するのであるが、現在残っている足利学校の建物は新しく、国内で最古の学
校建築はこの閑谷講堂となる。
閑谷講堂は、国宝に指定されている入母屋造の木造建築であるものの、簡素な造りであることに気がつく。
余計な造作は省かれており、組物はなく、柱の上には舟肘木が載せられ、それが桁を支えるばかりである。
もっと豪華な装飾が付加され、また立面や平面で複雑な技巧を凝らしている派手な日本建築は数多く存
在しているから、こういう地味な建築が、どうして国宝なのかと訝る向きもあるだろう。
長方形平面をなす室内には、円柱がちょうど10本立っている。その周囲には角柱が二重に並べられている。
ぐるりと板張りの廊下が周りに巡らされている形式である。日本のどこでも見られる平凡な建築であるよう
な気がするけれども、しかし一番外側に巡らされている角柱については、花頭窓の位置とそぐわない場所
に配されているところも見受けられる。もしくは花頭窓だけが並んでいて、床や棚や付書院などがまったく
ないのが奇異であると感じられるのかもしれない。こうした些細なところに留意しつつ、建物をゆっくりと
見ることを始めたい。
建物は遠くから眺めて四周を回り、まず外観を吟味し、次いで内部を観察するというのが基本と言われて
いるから、その順序で眺めることとしよう。幸いにしてこの建物の外側をぐるりと巡ることができ、また内観も
くまなく見通すことが可能である点は喜ばしい。まずは石塀に並行してその外側に長い池が掘られている
ことに気がつくが、これを泮池という。中国の規模の大きな教育施設では、四周が水を湛えた堀で囲まれ
ていた事実に基づいて、ここでも同じ構えが断片的に踏襲されていると考えられる。木造建築の傍らに池
を設けて水を常時用意しておくことは、また防火の上でも役立ったはずである。
長々と続く石塀に固く守られた敷地は広く、そこに講堂は建立されている。基本的に開放的な構成で、四周
に開かれた建物である。石塀越しに講堂の屋根を見ることができる。屋根瓦の色は黄赤を帯びている点
が独特で、これは現地産の土を使って焼いた備前焼による瓦を用いていることに起因する。人の目の高さ
を意識して積まれたであろう石塀の外と内とでは、わずかに高さを変えて内側の地面を上げており、敷地
内側から眺めた際の石塀の高さは若干低くなる。建物の内部からのほどよい視界も得ようとして、両引きの
障子を備える大きな花頭窓が並べられた。障子を開けると周囲の緑が鮮やかに目に映る。楷の木の枝ぶ
りも見事である。花頭窓が描く優美な曲線の輪郭は、たとえば京都の「慈照寺 銀閣」の上層に3つ並べら
れたものによく似ているようにも思われるが、この問題を解くにあたっては、他の建築遺構も含めたより詳し
い形の比較が必要だろう。
建物内部の板張りの床は異彩を放っている。丸い柱を立てて囲った内側と外側とで、高さをまったく変え
ていない。境には無目敷居を入れ、平滑に仕上げた床の全面に拭き漆を施している。最上の木材が選ば
れて建てられたことを明らかに証明するひとつがこの床面で、経年変化による目立った歪みや隙間が見ら

れない。磨き出されて黒く沈み込むように見える床面は、あたかも巨大な1枚の鏡であるかのように、この建物の柱や窓を反転させて映し出す。室内へ大事に格納されているように見える10本の円柱の姿とともに、内観の見どころとなっている。

学校と教育の始原

学校と呼ばれる建物の起源は、古代社会が成立した時と同じくらい古い。世界で最も古い学校の記録は、おそらく紀元前のシュメール文明に属するものにまで遡る[1]。現在のイラクに該当する箇所であり、ここには人類の古代社会を考える上で最も重要な都市遺跡群が集中している。楔形文字を用いて、当時のことを夥しい数の粘土板に書き残したこの文明の文字史料は、書記の養成のために読み書きを教える場が実際にあったこと、ウル第3王朝のシュルギ王（紀元前2094-47頃）が学校へ通い、算数が得意であったこと、また彼がシュメール語とアッカド語の筆記術を学んだことを伝えている。マリ王宮（紀元前2千年紀中葉）では、粘土で造られた長椅子がたくさん並んでいる部屋も見つかっており、これは学校の教室であるかもしれないと判断がなされている非常に特殊な遺構である。

シュメール文明の時代における教室で使われた教科書については、いまだに詳細がよくわかっていないが、生徒たちが学習内容に興味を持つように「謎々」の形式が用いられたと考えられている。教材にわかりやすさが加味されていたのではないかということであろう。学校のありさまと当時行なわれていた教育の方法、あるいはそこに集う学生や教員をテーマにした文字史料もいくらか残されている。断片的にしか伝わっていないため、しばしば推測によって大がかりな復原を行なうことが必要である点が残念ではある。だが、滅びてしまった古い言葉で書かれた次の文章は、現代に生きるわれわれにも生々しく響く。

「ぼくの先生は『君の文字は下手だ』といいました。そして先生はぼくを鞭で叩きました」[2]

字がきたない生徒が先生に叱られるこの話はこれで終わらない。この生徒から授業時の話を聞いた父は、先生を家に招いて歓待し、食事のもてなしを施すのである。ナツメヤシ酒をふるまい、新しい衣服もあてがった結果、先生はこの学生を褒めるまでに豹変する。情けない教員の話ではあるものの、しかし彼の愚かな身代わりの早さを書き留めているということは、古代においても倫理から外れた間違った行動を指摘することも含め、教育の方法が模索されていたとも推定することができるだろう。

古代エジプトでは、粘土板ではなく、パピルスという植物の繊維を薄く剥ぎ、叩いて圧着したものを筆記具に用いた。英語の「paper」の語源ともなっており、書記の養成のために用意されたパピルスの巻物の教科書がいくつか知られている。「書記という職業はこの世で最高である。この職業では汚れ作業に携わることがない」といった文面が書かれたものが残っており、高い教育を受けた書記という職務につくことが強く推奨された。しかし面白いのは、書記になろうとする学徒たちのどうしようもない怠惰の様子が別の場面では糾弾されている点で、「書記官が勉強嫌いの学童に与える忠告」として知られている「ランシング・パピルス(Papyrus Lansing)」では、「おまえの心は完成され、積み出されるばかりになった高さ百 尺^{キュビト}、厚さ十尺の大きな 碑^{オベリスク} よりも重い」[3]というように、あり得ないほど大きな1本石でできたオベリスクが引き合いに出されながら、生徒が容易に動かず、勉強への意欲を一向に示さないさまが活写されている。

「嫌味なパピルス(Satirical papyrus)」という別名を持つパピルスは、古代エジプトの建築や数学に関する著作において必ず触れられる文字史料であり、ひとりの書記が年若い見習いの書記に対して3つの建造作業に関わる問題を出すという構成を含んでいる。そこでは専門用語が多用され、素人にはほとんど内容が理解できない。その上、熟練の書記は勉強が途中の書記に対して早急に答えを出すことを強いている。ここには、シュメールで見られたわかりやすい教科書の書き方という側面がまったく見られない。平易な「謎々」で学生たちを解法に導くという方策はうかがわれず、一見、現場でなされている難解なやり方を、直截に初学者たちへぶつけるという方法を採用しているようである。だが、高飛車な教員の姿を描くことにより、ここでもまた間違った教員のあり方を面白おかしく見せようとしているのかもしれない。古代の教

1　小林登志子『シュメル：人類最古の文明』、中央公論新社、2005
2　前掲書、p. 210
3　杉勇 他「筑摩世界文学体系1：古代オリエント集」、筑摩書房、1978、p.646

科書をどう解釈するかは、いまだに憶測の域を超えていない。

学生はいつの時代でも怠け者であり、同時に旺盛な好奇心を持つ。こうしたなかで教育の基本的な理念とは、時代や地域を超えてほとんど変わらないように思われる。これは教育という、特殊な要素がそうさせるのではあるまいか。第一に、人は自分の知らないことを本当に教えることができない。この点で、教育は徹底して保守的である他はないという側面を必ず有する。第二に、教育の場で伝えようとすることとは、いつの時代にあっても革新性への不断の姿勢である。要するに試みられようとしている到達点が、出発点とは矛盾しており、またその矛盾をきたすことを第一義とするのである。

日本における学校建築として最古の例となる閑谷学校では、中国伝来の儒学が選ばれて教育が行なわれた。閑谷学校よりも時代が遡る足利学校においても、事情はほぼ似ていただろう。具体的には四書五経がこの場で素読されるのである。これらの教科書は紀元前に中国で成立し、高度な編纂がなされて紙に記された。これは学問というよりも、倫理あるいは生活の基盤とする考えと見なしたほうが近かった。人とは何か、という古くて新しいことが問われたわけである。そこでは古代の教科書で登場した無作法で乱暴な教員の意味が、分解されて教科書の行間に織り込まれている、そう見ても差し支えがないだろう。

講堂の建立とその後の変化

逆説的な書き方となるが、建物を見るにあたっては、いま自分が目にしている光景をそのまま信じるべきではない、という鉄則がある。現在のこの建物が建った時には、いまの楷の木はなかったし、またこの閑谷講堂の建設を命じた備前岡山藩主の池田光政 (1609-82) もすでに亡くなっていた。池田が津田永忠 (1640-1707) を呼んで閑谷学校を造らせた時、講堂は草葺きで、瓦では葺かれていなかった。備前焼の瓦が載せられた再建の講堂は、池田の死後に完成する。楷の木は、学問の木、あるいは孔子木とも呼ばれるが、これは儒学の始祖である孔子 (紀元前551-479頃) の墓に植えられていたことに因む。今、見られるのは大正時代に植えられた木である。閑谷講堂の東面に位置する花頭窓の障子を開け放つと、そこから素晴らしい木の形姿を眺めることができることはすでに記した。かつては存在したがいまはないもの、そしてかつてはなかったがいまは存在するものが、ない混ぜの状態になっている。たいてい世のなかはこのような状態であり、学問というものはその正しい順序通りに並べて理解することを目指している。講堂の建立の発端から見ていくこととしよう。

池田光政は役目上、領内を見て回ることを続けているうちに、気に入った場所を見出した。日本は小さな島国で、北東から南西に向かって長く伸び、山地が国土の2/3を占める。川は短く、急流であることが多い。池田光政が治世を行なった岡山の地でも、水の対策に頭を悩ます事態がしばしば発生した。地層が水平に重なっているところはこの国では珍しく、褶曲が広い範囲で観察される。だが言い換えるならば、これは変化に富む国土であることを意味し、少し歩けばすぐに風景が変わって人々の目を楽しませた。江戸時代の道中記を研究している者は、このありさまを「細長い観光地、テーマパーク」[4]に喩えているほどである。道中記とは、平たく言えば戦国時代が終わって国が安定したあとに流行した旅のガイドブックで、多種多様なものが刊行された。この時代にこれほど多くのガイドブックが出されたのは世界でも例がない。ガイドブックの普及の次には、優良宿屋と連携し、荷物を次の宿場に運ぶサービスなどが考え出された。瀬戸内海は代表的な景勝地であって、往来も非常に多かったであろう。そうした賑わいを見せる人気の場所とは遠く離れた閑静な場所に、池田光政は心の安らぎを覚えたらしく思われる。「閑谷」という地名は、まさに光政がこの土地に感応した思いが表わされたことに因んで与えられた。

本当は自分や一族の墓所をどこに造るべきかを探しあてようともしていたのであったが、低い山間の場所は好ましく感じられ、また庶民師弟の教育の場としても適していると考えて、彼は藩士の津田永忠に、この場所へ学校を建設することを命じた。津田永忠は有能な部下であって、岡山の「後楽園」[図1]の造営においても腕を奮った。さらには、今で言う土木工学の専門知識も持っていた石工の河内屋治兵衛(生没年

---

4 山本光正「旅から旅行へ——近世・近代の旅行史とその課題——」、『交通史研究60』、交通史研究会、2006、pp.1-16

不明)が配下におり、彼が有する技術は津田によって多様に駆使された。

選ばれた閑谷の敷地は、かなりの改造と修景がなされている点に留意する必要がある。選地はそのまま使われたわけではなく、まず山裾が削られて広い平地が確保された。中国に由来する四神相応に見合った整備も、もちろん考えに含められていたはずである。同時に瓦を焼くための陶土の確保と、石塀で用いるための石材の切り出しも考慮されていたと考えられる。工事現場で建材が調達できるのであれば、建設作業においては最も有利であった。

講堂は削られた山裾の近くに建てられ、南側に大きく余地を残すように配置されている。削られた山裾から出る石のいくばくかは石塀に転用がなされただろう。山が迫っている北側の花頭窓の障子から入ってくる光は、緑に覆われている山裾の影響を受けて、他とは異なる色合いを呈する。表情を変える光を四方から取り入れる箱として、この講堂は造られている点が注目される。

図1｜撮影=小川重雄

寸法計画と「ずれ」

講堂の中央(身舎)を占める梁間2間、桁行3間を構成する10本の円柱は、梁行と桁行とで微妙に柱間が異なっている。円柱による梁行2間という構成は、日本建築の古い住宅形式を思い起こさせ、見る者に歴史的な連想を誘惑してやまない。円柱は角柱よりも歴史的に古い形式である。円柱に関わる日本建築史を遡るならば、それは中国の宮殿建築の形をどう真似するかに始終したといっても過言ではないだろう。さらには矩形平面を形づくるときに、短辺すなわち梁行を2間にするという計画方法は、寝殿造と呼ばれる日本の古代の貴族住宅の形式であり、それを思い出させることとなる。

昭和の修理工事報告書[5]には、この円柱の太さは掲載されていない。許可を得て実測したところ、直径は253mmほどと判明した。この値は5/6尺を意味すると思われる。なお、角柱については202mm前後を測り、これは2/3尺の太さであると考えられる。柱の大きさが1尺の5/6や2/3となっている点も、円柱部分の建築の計画方法の古さを感じさせるひとつの要因である。建物の基本的な大きさを、当時用いられていた物差しの長さの切りのよい倍数、あるいはその物差しより短い場合には、その1/2や1/3、あるいはその組合せなどによる簡単な割合で規定しようとする傾向は、古代世界でしばしば観察されるからである。

だが、柱間に関してもこれに準じた計画方法が予想されるかといえば裏切られるのであって、各間の寸法はこれに対応していない。各間の寸法は、柱の太さの単純な倍数にはなっていないのである。

この建物では疎垂木が採用されており、おそらく垂木の歩みは最外周に並ぶ柱の各間で微妙に異なる計画となっていると思われる。これがこの建物の大きな特色である。建物の中央部では円柱が古代的な様相をうかがわせるが、周囲の角柱の配置は近世の技術の達成度を典型的に表しており、柱筋のずれが露わである。閑谷講堂は学校建築であるから、多数の学生を収容できる屋内空間の確保だけを目的とした建造物である。そこには、空間秩序の上下といった一切の配慮がなされておらず、裸の構造形式がただ晒されているような案配となっている。中心から外へと向かう空間の移動は、同時に時間軸における旅行ともなって

5　岡山県教育委員会『特別史蹟並びに国宝及び重要文化財 閑谷黌講堂外四棟保存修理(第一期)工事報告書』、岡山県教育委員会、1961

いる点が示唆されているのであり、興味深い。

身舎の2間の柱間についてはそれぞれ内々で2,740mmほどで、これに柱の太さ253mmを足せば2,993mmとなり、これが柱心々の距離となる。

疎垂木の配り方は、最も外側に位置する角柱の柱間を桁行・梁行方向の双方とも5つに均等割とするが、桁行方向では5つの柱間にそれぞれ14の枝割を与え、また梁間方向では11枝を配る。同じ幅で四周を巡る縁には6枝が与えられている。縁における隅の間では庇の隅柱の位置との関わりが重要で、庇の隅柱の心と垂木の心が一致する。角柱の間に配られる垂木の間隔は実際には異なるが、大まかに見れば等しいように目立たなくした工夫が見られる。

柱筋がずれているにもかかわらず、その上に載せられた重い屋根を支えることができているのは、日本建築が江戸時代までに屋根の架構方法を練り上げたからである。縦横に木を組んで立体的に支え、また、要所にはてこの原理を利用して、軒の先を上へ持ち上げた。この方法は日本で独自に開発されたものであり、屋根の自由な造形を語る際には特筆される。閑谷講堂に施されたこうした工夫は、天井が張られているので見ることができない。だが柱筋を通すことを第一に考える必要がなくなって、柱配置の比較的自由な想定が可能となった歴史が、この隠された屋根の部分にあるのだと見ておくことは重要である。

石積みと治水、防水と防火の技術

閑谷講堂をはじめとして、主要な建物を不思議な石塀が囲い込んでいる。かまぼこ型を呈するこのような石積みの形を世界の石造史に見出そうとするならば、まずはエジプトのピラミッドの周囲で見られる外周壁が思い起こされるであろう。今日では多くが失われ、第5王朝に属するサフラー王（紀元前25世紀頃）のピラミッドの周囲のものがかろうじて残るに過ぎないが、形はよく似ていても、石の積み方はまったく異なっている。

石の形はひとつとして同じではなく、また目地が直線状に仕上げられていない。ヨーロッパでの切石を積む方法とは、明らかに異質である。日本の石垣などでは、しばしばこのような石組みに出会うことがある。だがヨーロッパにこうしたものが皆無であるとは言えない。例えばギリシャのデルフィには、石目地が曲線を描いている似た組積を見ることができる[6]。アジアにおける石造建築へと目を移すならば、スリランカの「リティガラ遺跡」[図2]などで見ることが可能である。目地が直線状に整えられた組積方法についてはよく情報が整理されており、石造建築研究の主流となっているが、そこから外れた石の組み方に関しては、今後の研究の進展を待たなくてはならないだろう。

図2｜撮影=西本真一

土木、特に治水の方法を駆使した者が工事に関わっていたことを考える時、時代が降るものの、和歌山の「水軒堤防」などとの関連も予想される。

この石塀によって学校の敷地の全体を囲い込むことは、他方で、ここに降り込んできた雨水の逃げ場を失わせることにもつながる。それを避けるため、囲まれた平地には山裾から南に向かって並行した溝が多数

---

6 Marie-Christine Hellmann, *L'architecture grecque 1: Les principes de la construction* [Greek Architecture, vol. 1, Principles of Construction] (Paris: Picard, 2002) 5.

掘られ、石塀の下を通って排水ができるように考えられた。つまり閑谷講堂は、治水事業と木質架構技術との高度な合体を示している。

木造建築の大敵と言えば、もちろん火と水であった。講堂の切妻が漆喰の塗り込めとされているのも、火を恐れてのことであったろう。この仕上げは外観に重厚さをもたらしているが、最初の草葺きから再建時に備前焼の瓦葺きへと変更されたのも、防火を意識した可能性が指摘される。聖廟の屋根で用いられていた瓦の裏側に「天下一御瓦」と記されたものも発見されており[7]、瓦を製造した職人たちは自分らの手掛けるこの建物に大きな誇りを持っていたに違いない。

木でできた建物を滅ぼす要因として、火と同じく水を遠ざけようとした証拠が残っている。屋根を見上げるならば、軒先に小さな管が並んで突出していることに気づく。このような意匠は他の日本建築ではまったく見ることができない。解体調査の結果、入念な防水工事が屋根面になされていた点が判明した。小さな管は、万一備前焼の瓦の下に水が入ったときに、それを集めて排出するための備前焼による陶製の排出口であり、厳重な板葺きの上に、さらに紙が貼られるなど、尋常ではない対策が幾重にも施されていた。

日本建築において、建物の保存を考えた結果、水を遠ざけるいくつかの方法はあり得る。縁の隅には豆腐板を置き、濡れることが多い縁の隅部が傷んだ場合の交換の簡便さを狙うといった伝統上の意匠でも確認することができよう。しかしここで見られる建物を永く持たせるための工夫とは、これまで誰もやろうとしたことのなかった保存の方法である。講堂が建つ地面から水を抜く大規模な構法との関連を見ることもできよう。しかも、その工夫の跡はここでもまったく見ることができず、隠された部分に適用されている。

岡山における石の加工技術の進展とその蓄積は、元々良質な石がこの地で採掘できるという恵まれた環境のもとに育まれた。重い石材の運搬を円滑に進めるには、船による運搬が適しているが、瀬戸内海という穏やかな環境が同時に与えられ、江戸時代に至ると土地の開墾や埋め立てに伴う作業によって、さらに技術が整えられたと見ることができる。この土地が持つ潜在力が、ここに住む者たちによって花開いたのであった。

講堂の建築には、その知恵の蓄積を前提とする工夫が重ねられていると見るべきである。

雨戸に見る特異性

雨戸には戸車が仕込まれており、開閉が容易になるよう工夫されている。通常よりもしっかりと造られた雨戸となっている。

『国宝大事典5：建造物』で閑谷講堂が掲載されている頁[8]においては、この建物の4面を巡る雨戸に関して触れられている。この種の短い解説のなかで、雨戸について言及されている建築遺構というのは珍しい。毎日、雨戸が閉められるという簡単な内容であるのだが、4面の雨戸が閉じた閑谷講堂の姿が、また実に印象深いことをこの文は伝えようとしているように思われる。

「小斎」と呼ばれる小さな建物が、講堂の南面に建てられている。ここは藩主が時折立ち寄って、講堂の様子を眺めるための施設である。屋根には瓦を置かず、東屋風の質素な佇まいを示し、藩主のための建物としては異例に思われるものの、教育の場にあって意図的に権威者の控えた姿勢を示そうとしたとも考えられる。

ここにも閑谷講堂と同様の、戸車付きの雨戸が見られるが、東面には戸袋がなく、省略されている。小斎の東面に立て込まれる雨戸は、北東の隅柱のところで90度回され、北面に並ぶ雨戸と一緒にひとつの戸袋の内へ収められるのである。座敷からの眺めを大切にするとき、「雨戸廻し」と呼ばれるこうした工夫が雨戸に施された。後楽園の主要な建築であった「延養亭」は、残念なことに戦災によって失われたが、現在では復原されており、広い庭を見渡すために柱を少なくし、雨戸の戸袋を同様になくしているさまを見ることができる。

同じ後楽園に建つ名建築の「流店」[図3]は、吹き放ちのただなかに小川の流れを挿入するという大胆な建物であるが、上層が設けられており、ここからも四周の広大な庭を楽しむことができた。上の階の部屋に設けられた横長の窓の雨戸のための戸袋を消すことはしていないが、位置は半分建物から飛び出したか

---

7 岡山県教育委員会『特別史蹟並びに国宝及び重要文化財 閑谷黌聖廟、閑谷神社々殿及び石塀保存修理（第二期）工事報告書』、岡山県教育委員会、1962, p. 42

8 鈴木嘉吉編『国宝大事典5：建造物』、講談社、1985, p.465

たちで備えられており、別の工夫の痕跡がうかがわれる。

明治末に建てられた「濱口家住宅 御風楼」（和歌山県）は、客をもてなすための座敷が3階に広がるが、ここでは驚くべきことに、雨戸を格納したあとに、その戸袋を鉄鎖で下階へ降ろすという工夫がなされている。この例は極端であろうが、日本建築において眺めを最優先に考えた場合、視覚的に邪魔になる柱や戸袋をなくす工夫を、日本人がどのように展開させていったかを知る上で興味が惹かれる。

閑谷講堂では、戸袋の数を減らそうとは考えられなかった。4つの各面に戸袋を配置するという常套手段を変えるつもりがなかったことを意味する。ただし、西面を除く各面の中央には階段が配されており、その位置にあたる雨戸には潜戸を付加するように造られた。普通は一間に2枚の雨戸が割り当てられるであろう。しかしここでは、中央間に潜戸を備える雨戸がなければならない。従って、雨戸の幅は最外周の柱間を考慮せずに定められている。こういう些細な点にも、この建物の計画の面白さがうかがわれる。

正面の中央にぽつんと戸口を示すモニュメンタルな日本建築ということなら、正倉院が代表的であろうか。正倉院の重要性は誰もが知っており、ここは古くからの重要な遺物を守る蔵である。一方、閑谷講堂の内部は空で、具体的に目に見えるものを守る施設ではない。

ここはおそらく、思想や歴史を重ねた知恵を長く収蔵することを願った箱であり、同時に光を考えた箱である。ただし室内からの景観はあまり考慮されることはなかった。人の目が感知する風景の素晴らしさよりも、まずこの箱に差し込む光が考慮された箱であった。また長く時間に耐えることができるよう、入念に考えられて造られた箱であったように思われる。

夕刻、からからから……、と閑谷講堂の雨戸がすべて閉ざされ、この建物はあたかも屋根が載せられた大きな箱のような姿へと変貌する[図4]。陽光はほぼ遮断されて、昼間とは異なり、暗箱へと転ずる。この写真集で被写体となっている閑谷講堂は、それ自体が大きな「カメラ・オブスクラ：暗い部屋」でもあり、床面には鏡も隠し持っている。たぶん偶然ではないその重層性について、最後に言い添えておく。

謝辞
溝口明則・小岩正樹両氏による御協力に心から感謝申し上げたい。

図3｜撮影=小川重雄

図4｜雨戸が閉じられた閑谷学校 講堂
撮影=富井雄太郎

［参考文献］

- 岡山県教育委員会『特別史蹟並びに国宝及び重要文化財 閑谷黌講堂外四棟保存修理（第一期）工事報告書』、岡山県教育委員会、1961
- 岡山県教育委員会『特別史蹟並びに国宝及び重要文化財 閑谷黌聖廟、閑谷神社々殿及び石塀保存修理（第二期）工事報告書』、岡山県教育委員会、1962
- 小林登志子『シュメル：人類最古の文明』、中央公論新社、2005
- 齋藤裕『日本建築の形II』、TOTO出版、2017
- 澤田名垂「家屋雑考」、故実叢書編集部『新訂増補故実叢書：鳳闕見聞図説・安政御造営記・宮殿調度沿革・調度図会・室町殿屋形私考・家屋雑考・服飾管見』、明治図書出版、初出：1842（天保13）、新訂：1951、pp. 221-316
- 鈴木嘉吉編『国宝大事典5：建造物』、講談社、1985
- 藤森照信・山口晃『日本建築集中講義』、淡交社、2013
- 藤森照信・藤塚光政『日本木造遺産：千年の建築を旅する』、世界文化社、2014
- 光井渉『日本の伝統木造建築：その空間と構法』、市ヶ谷出版社、2016
- 杉勇 他「筑摩世界文学体系1：古代オリエント集」、筑摩書房、1978
- Aylward M. Blackman and T. Eric Peet, "Papyrus Lansing: A Translation with Notes." *Journal of Egyptian Archaeology* 11, no. 3–4 (1925): 284–298.
- Marie-Christine Hellmann, *L'architecture grecque 1: Les principes de la construction* [Greek Architecture, vol. 1, Principles of Construction], Paris: Picard, 2002
- Ricardo Augusto Caminos, Late-Egyptian Miscellanies. Brown Egyptological Studies 1, London : Oxford University Press, 1954

A Wooden Box Containing the Wisdom of the Ages | Shin'ichi Nishimoto

In the morning, the wooden shutters of the Shizutani School lecture hall slide open with a clatter, allowing the sun to pour in through its rows of bell-shaped windows.

The Shizutani lecture hall is the oldest existing school building in Japan. Although Tochigi prefecture's Ashikaga Gakkō school is said to have been established as far back as the medieval period and was mentioned in sixteenth-century correspondence from Francisco Xavier (1506–1552), its current school buildings are new.

Built of wood with a hip-and-gable roof, the Shizutani lecture hall is noticeably plain in construction. Omitting any unnecessary fittings, the building has no bracket complexes, supporting the purlins instead with simple boat-shaped bracket arms atop its pillars. Given that there are so many striking examples of Japanese architecture that are more splendidly embellished, or that reveal complex and ingenious techniques in their plans and elevations, one may wonder why this modest structure was chosen as a designated national treasure.

The rectangular interior floor plan has ten round pillars at its center that are surrounded by two rings of square pillars, creating a single central room enclosed on all sides by a wooden-floored veranda. Although at first glance this seems like an ordinary sort of building that might be found anywhere in Japan, the outermost pillars do seem out of step with the building's bell-shaped windows. Perhaps what feels odd is that the bell-shaped windows appear without the alcoves, staggered shelves, and built-in writing tables that ordinarily accompany them in *shoin-zukuri* style residential architecture. Taking note of such details, I would like now to take a closer look.

My general approach is to circle a building from a distance to examine its exterior from all sides before going inside, and that is the order I will follow here. Fortunately, it is possible to go all the way around the outside of the lecture hall and also to look everywhere in the interior. The first thing one notices is the long pond, called a *hanchi*, dug parallel to and just outside the stone walls. This seems to follow, if incompletely, the Chinese practice of surrounding large educational institutions with water-filled moats. Providing an ever-ready source of water in the form of a pond near the wooden building must also have been helpful in terms of fire prevention.

The lecture hall stands on expansive grounds firmly protected by long stone walls. The layout is fundamentally an open one with the building exposed on all sides. The roof of the lecture hall can be seen over the stone walls, the distinctive yellowish red of its tiles stemming from the use of local clay fired in the Bizen style. The ground on either side of the stone walls, surely designed with an appreciation for the height of the human eye, varies slightly in elevation; that on the inside is raised such that the walls feels lower when seen from within than when seen from without. To ensure a pleasant view from inside, the building has rows of large bell-shaped windows provided with double sliding shoji screens that can be opened to the surrounding greenery, including magnificent Chinese pistachio trees. The elegantly curved outline of the bell-shaped windows bears a striking similarity to that of the ones found in rows of three on the upper level of the Silver Pavilion at Jishō-ji temple in Kyoto. Solving this riddle, however, probably requires a more detailed comparison encompassing other architectural works as well.

The wooden floor of the building interior gives off a conspicuous shine. Within and beyond the round pillars at the core there is no variation at all in the height of the floor. A level threshold marks the border while the entire floor, smooth and flat, is coated with a wiped-lacquer finish. Clearly demonstrating that the finest timber was used in the building's construction, the floor shows no apparent warping or gaps due to age. The polished, deep black surface of the floor reflects the building's pillars and windows like a single massive mirror. It is a highlight of the interior, as are the ten round pillars themselves, which the building seems almost to have been designed to contain.

The Origins of Schools and Education

The origins of schools go back as far as the days when ancient societies were formed. The world's oldest record of a school probably dates back to the Sumer civilization before the start of the Common Era.[1] The most important group of urban ruins for thinking about ancient human society can be found concentrated

1 Toshiko Kobayashi, *Shumeru: jinrui saiko no bunmei* [Sumer: Mankind's Oldest Civilization](Chūo Kōronsha, 2005).

in a location corresponding to modern Iraq. Written documents from this civilization, which employed cuneiform characters to record contemporary matters on massive numbers of clay tablets, relay that there were places for teaching reading and writing to train scribes, that King Shulgi (2094–2047 BCE) of the Third Dynasty of Ur attended school and excelled at mathematics, and that he learned to write in both Sumerian and Akkadian. Rooms with many rows of benches made of clay have been found at the Royal Palace of Mari (mid-2nd millennium BCE), an unusual construction provisionally identified as classrooms.

Although details about the textbooks used in classrooms at the time of the Sumer civilization remain unclear, they are thought to have taken the form of riddles as a way to keep students interested in the subjects being taught. Materials surely must also have been designed for ease of comprehension. Some written documents also describe the schools and teaching methods of the day or discuss the students and teachers who gathered there. It is unfortunate that the fragmentary nature of such records means their full reconstruction often requires leaps of the imagination, but the following text, originally written in a dead and ancient tongue, rings all too clearly in our ears today: "My teacher said, 'Your letters are atrocious,' and struck me with a cane."[2]

But this tale of a student scolded by his teacher for ill-formed letters does not end here. When he tells his father this episode from class, the father invites his teacher to their home, welcoming him warmly and treating him to a meal. After being served date wine and provided with new clothes, the teacher does a complete reversal and begins praising the student. Although this is deplorable conduct for a teacher, the fact that the speed of his foolish turnaround was recorded suggests that even in ancient times efforts to identify proper teaching methods included taking note of unethical and mistaken behavior.

In ancient Egypt, writing was done not on clay tablets but rather on thin strips of fiber from the stalk of the papyrus plant that were beaten and bonded under pressure. The English word "paper" comes from papyrus. A number of known papyrus scrolls were used as textbooks for training of scribes. Some serve as a strong recommendation for the job of an educated scribe, offering that, "A scribe is the greatest profession in the world, an occupation in which there is no dirty work." Interestingly, however, in other places such prospective scribes are censured for their incurable indolence. The Papyrus Lansing, describing advice given by a scribe to a student who dislikes studying, reads, "Thy heart is heavier than a great monument of a hundred cubits in height and ten in thickness, which is finished and ready for loading."[3] Invoking an obelisk made from an impossibly large slab of stone, it vividly describes a student who is not easily moved and shows not the least interest in his studies.

Writings on ancient Egyptian architecture and mathematics invariably mention a satirical papyrus that, in part, takes the form of a master scribe presenting a young trainee with questions about three works of architecture. The master scribe uses many technical terms that would be all but incomprehensible to lay people and pushes his student, still only midway through his studies, to provide answers immediately.

Here there is none of the ease of comprehension found in Sumerian textbooks. Rather than simple riddles designed to lead students to an understanding of how to solve problems, it seems to adopt the method of confronting beginners directly with difficult-to-understand practical problems. It may, however, have been an effort to humorously illustrate mistaken teaching methods by depicting an overbearing instructor. Alas, the interpretation of ancient textbooks remains a speculative endeavor.

Students are lazy in any age, and yet also incredibly curious. In this sense, the fundamental principles of education are, I think, essentially the same across time and place. Is this not due to certain elements intrinsic to education? First, people are unable to really teach what they do not themselves know. In this sense, education inevitably has a fundamentally conservative aspect. Second, educational forums in every age seek to convey a posture of constant innovation. In other words, the goal being aimed for is inconsistent with the starting point, and the most important thing is to recognize this contradiction.

At the Shizutani School, the oldest example of school architecture in Japan, Confucianism introduced from China was chosen as the subject to be taught. The situation was surely much the same at the older Ashikaga Gakkō. Specifically, readings were conducted of the Four Books and Five Classics, textbooks established in China before the start of the Common Era, thoroughly edited, and recorded on paper. It would be best to view them less as works of scholarship than as descriptions of ethics or a philosophy that forms a foundation for living. They address the eternal question of man's identity. Surely there can be nothing wrong with seeing in them the significance of the ill-mannered and unreasonable teachers who appear in ancient textbooks, thoroughly broken down and incorporated between the lines.

<u>Construction of the Lecture Hall and Later Developments</u>

Although it may seem paradoxical, there is an ironclad rule that when looking at a building you should never take what appears before your eyes at face value. The Chinese pistachio trees that stands on the grounds of the Shizutani lecture hall were not there when the current building was constructed, and Ikeda Mitsumasa (1609–1682), the lord of the Okayama domain who ordered it built, had already passed away. When Ikeda had Tsuda Nagatada (1640–1707) build the Shizutani School, the original lecture hall was roofed with

---

2 Ibid., 210.

3 Isamu Sugi, et al., *Chikuma sekai bungaku taikei 1: kodai ejiputo shū* [Chikuma World Literature Series, vol.1, Ancient Egypt] (Chikuma Shobō, 1978), 646.

thatch, not tiles. The reconstructed lecture hall with its Bizen ware roof tiles was not completed until after Ikeda's death. The Chinese pistachio is known as the "tree of learning" or the "Confucius tree" because it was planted at the grave of Confucius (c. 551–479 BCE), the founder of Confucianism. The trees seen today were planted during the Taishō period (1912–1926). I mentioned above that opening the shoji screens in the bell-shaped windows on the east face of the lecture hall reveals a wonderful view of the magnificently shaped trees. Generally speaking, the world is an interwoven mix of things that once were but are no longer and things that never existed before but do now, and scholarship aims to understand things by placing these in the proper order. Let's start by looking at the impetus for the construction of the lecture hall.

While touring his domain as part of his official duties, Ikeda Mitsumasa discovered a location that he liked very much. Japan is a small island nation stretching in a long, narrow line from the northeast to the southwest. Two-thirds of its territory is covered in mountains. Rivers are short and often quickly moving. The Okayama area where Ikeda ruled frequently struggled with water-related issues. There are few places in Japan where geological strata are layered horizontally, while geological folds are widely observed. Put another way, this means the country has richly varied terrain, and walking just a short distance beings a change to the scenery that delights the eyes. So much so, in fact, that a scholar of Edo-period *dōchūki* travelers' journals has described the country as being like a "long, narrow tourist area or theme park."[4] In simplest terms, such journals—which were published in enormous variety—served as popular travel guidebooks during the time of national stability that followed the end of the war-torn Sengoku period. Nowhere else in the world were so many such guidebooks produced during that era. After the spread of such guidebooks, people came up with the idea of a service linked to reputable lodgings that would deliver luggage from one post town to the next. Renowned for its scenic beauty, the Setó Inland Sea was no doubt heavily trafficked. Ikeda seems to have found solace in quiet areas far from such popular, bustling location, and named this spot Shizutani ("tranquil valley") as an expression of his emotional response to the land.

Although Ikeda was actually searching for a burial site for himself and his family, he liked this spot nestled among low hills, thought it well-suited to serve as a place for educating commoners, and ordered his vassal Tsuda Nagatada to construct a school there. Tsuda was a talented fellow who would later demonstrate his abilities in constructing the Kōraku-en garden [Fig. 1] in Okayama. Tsuda also made full use of the skills of stonemason Kawachiya Jihei (dates unknown), a subordinate with expert knowledge of what today would be called civil engineering.

It is important to note that the chosen site in Shizutani underwent significant alterations and landscaping. Rather than using the site as it was found, the foothills were carved away to secure a broad expanse of level ground. Such improvements were no doubt made under the influence of *shijin sōō*, a concept that originated in China of an ideal topography corresponding to the four Taoist gods. It is presumed, too, that securing a source of clay for firing roof tiles and the need to quarry stone for the surrounding walls were also taken into consideration. After all, the most advantageous situation when constructing something is to be able to procure the materials on site.

The lecture hall was built near the carved away foothills, positioned to leave a wide expanse of empty space to the south. Some portion of the excavated material must surely have been put to use in constructing the stone walls. Light coming in through the bell-shaped windows' shoji on the building's north side, influenced by the greenery that covers the encroaching hills, is tinted differently than what arrives from other directions. Notably, the lecture hall was built as a box that lets in light of a different cast from each of its four sides.

Fig. 1 | Photo by Shigeo Ogawa

Misalignment in Dimensional Planning

The ten round pillars that form the three-bay-wide, two-bay-deep core of the lecture hall are arranged such that the distance between the pillars varies somewhat in the longitudinal and transverse directions. The two-

---

4 Mitsumasa Yamamoto, "Tabi kara ryokō e: kinsei kindai no ryokōshi to sono kadai" [From Journey to Trip: The History of Travel in the Early Modern and Modern Periods], *Kōtsūshi Kenkyū* 60 (The Japanese Society of the History of Transport and Communications, 2006), 1–16.

bay deep structure is reminiscent of ancient Japanese residential architecture and invites the viewer to indulge in historical associations. Round pillars are historically older than square pillars, and it would not be overstating things to suggest that the history of Japanese architecture as it relates to round pillars begins and ends with how to imitate the forms of Chinese palace architecture. In addition, the building reminds us that when creating a rectangular floor plan, planning the short side—that is, the transverse side—to be two bays deep was a characteristic of the *shinden-zukuri* style of ancient Japanese residential aristocratic architecture.

The thickness of the round pillars is not mentioned in the report summarizing the repairs to the building made during the Showa period.[5] I received permission to measure them myself and found them to be about 253 millimeters in diameter, a value corresponding to 5/6 of a *shaku*. The square pillars measured about 202 millimeters in thickness, or about 2/3 of a *shaku*. That the thickness of the pillars is 5/6 or 2/3 of a *shaku* suggests ancient origins for the methods by which the structure was planned. In the ancient world there was a tendency to prescribe a building's basic sizes according to simple proportions, either as multiples of the length of the unit of measure then employed, fractions thereof such as 1/2 or 1/3, or a combination of the two.

We might, then, imagine that the intervals between pillars would also be planned in a similar fashion, but here our expectations are betrayed as the distances between pillars are not simple multiples of their thickness.

The lecture hall employs widely spaced rafters whose spacing seems to vary among the bays along the outermost ring of pillars, a major distinguishing characteristic of the building. At the center of the building the round pillars suggest an ancient aspect, but the positioning of the square pillars on the periphery is a classic expression of early modern technical achievement, one in which the misalignment in the rows of pillars is openly exposed. Given the Shizutani lecture hall's function as school architecture, its primary objective was to secure an interior space that could hold a large number of students. In this there is no consideration given for a hierarchy of spatial order, and the arrangement bares the building's naked structural form. It is fascinating that the spatial shift from center to periphery also suggests a journey along a temporal continuum.

The distance between the pillars along the two transverse bays of the core is about 2,740 millimeters; adding the 253-millimeter diameter of the pillars themselves gives a distance of 2,993 millimeters between the center of one pillar and the center of the next.

Returning to the arrangement of the rafters, the outermost ring of pillars divides the building into five bays on each side, with 14 rafters along each longitudinal bay and 11 along each transverse bay (the building is wider than it is deep). The veranda maintains a constant width on all four sides of the building, with 6 rafters allocated throughout. The relationship of the veranda corners to the corners of the middle ring of pillars is critical, through, so here the centers of the rafters are aligned with the centers of the pillars. This causes the rafter intervals elsewhere to vary, but things are arranged in such a way that the spacing appears roughly equal.

That the heavy roof is capable of being supported despite the misalignment of the pillars is the result of improvements made to roof framing methods in Japanese architecture prior to the Edo period. Three-dimensional support provided through a combination of vertical and horizontal timbers, and the application of the principle of leverage at strategic points, was used to lift up the tips of the rafters. Developed independently in Japan, this method deserves special mention when discussing the freeform shape of roofs. The Shizutani lecture hall ceiling conceals how such contrivances were applied, but it is important to note that this hidden section of the roof holds a history of how being freed from the need to prioritize aligning the rows of pillars opened up new, relatively unconstrained possibilities for positioning them.

<u>Masonry and Flood Control, Waterproofing and Fire-prevention</u>

The Shizutani lecture hall and the school's other principal buildings are enclosed by rather unusual stone walls. Searching for similar examples of such semi-cylindrical stone walls elsewhere in the world, I am first reminded of the enclosure walls surrounding Egyptian pyramids. Today most of these have been lost, with what remains being found at the Pyramid of Sahure, a pharaoh of the fifth dynasty (about mid-25th century BCE). The shape is quite similar, but the method of stacking the stones is completely different.

No two stones have the same shape and their joints are not finished in straight lines. This is clearly unlike the European method of stacking stone blocks. Such stacking is frequently encountered in the stone walls of Japan and not entirely unknown in Europe. Similar masonry with curved joints between stones can be seen, for example, at Delphi in Greece.[6] Turning to stone architecture in Asia, it can also be seen at the ruins of the Ritigala monastery Fig.2 in Sri Lanka. Information about masonry methods in which the joints between stones are arranged in straight lines is well organized and makes up the mainstream of scholarship on stone architecture, but with respect to methods of stacking stone that deviate from this I'm afraid we must wait for advances in future research.

That experts in civil engineering—and flood control methods in particular—were involved in building the Shizutani School suggests some relationship to structures such as the Suiken Dike in Wakayama, although this was built rather earlier.

Encircling the entire grounds of the school with stone walls could deprive them of a means to allow rainwater to drain away. To avoid this, a number of ditches were provided running parallel through the

---

5 Okayama Prefectural Board of Education, *Tokubetsu shiseki narabi ni kokuhō oyobi jūyō bunkazai shizutani kō kōdō hoka yontō hozon shūri (dai ikki) kōji hōkokusho* [Report on the Conservation and Repair (First Phase) of Special Historical Site, National Treasure, and Important Cultural Property Shizutani School Lecture Hall and Four Outbuildings] (Okayama Prefectural Board of Education, 1961).

6 Marie-Christine Hellmann, *L'architecture grecque 1: Les principes de la construction* [Greek Architecture, vol. 1, Principles of Construction]

enclosed grounds from the foothills to the north through the level ground to the south. These pass beneath the walls, permitting rainwater to escape. The Shizutani lecture hall, then, is a high-level combination of advanced wood framing techniques and flood control methods.

Fig. 2 | Photo by Shin'ichi Nishimoto

The great enemies of wooden construction, of course, are fire and water. Covering the gables of the lecture hall with plaster was surely a means of preventing the spread of fire, and also brings a sense of massiveness and depth to the exterior. It has been noted that the change in roofing materials from thatch to Bizen ware tiles made when the structure was rebuilt may also have been undertaken with a mind to fire prevention. The underside of one of the tiles used on the roof of the Confucian temple was found to contain the inscription *tenkaichi onkawara* ["finest roof tiles in the land"],[7] suggesting the pride that the craftsmen who produced them took in working on the school buildings.

There is evidence that water was just as feared a threat to a building made of wood as fire. If you look up at the roof of the lecture hall you will notice rows of small pipes protruding from the rafters. Such a design is never seen in other Japanese architecture. When the building was dismantled for research and repair it was discovered that the surface of the roof had been subjected to elaborate waterproofing techniques. The small pipes, made of Bizen earthenware, were designed to collect and drain any water that managed the find its way under the roof tiles, while a paper covering had also been applied over the securely fixed wooden shingles beneath. In this way, the measures taken were both extraordinary and multi-layered.

When thinking about how to preserve a building, Japanese architecture offers a number of possible ways to keep water away. One example is traditional designs that place easily replaced "tofu boards" on the corners of exposed verandas, since corners are most frequently damaged by exposure to water. The Shizutani lecture hall, however, adopted ingenious methods of long-term preservation that no one had ever attempted before. These may also be related to the extensive efforts made to drain the land on which the building stands. What is more, evidence of the efforts is all but invisible as they were applied to areas that are concealed.

Advances in stone processing techniques were cultivated and accumulated in Okayama because it was a place where quality stones could be quarried locally. Shipping is ideal for transporting heavy stones over distance and the Seto Inland Sea offered a relatively tranquil environment for doing so. By the Edo period, land reclamation and cultivation projects led to further refinements in technology and the latent strengths of the area blossomed due to the efforts of the people who lived there.

The architecture of the lecture hall and its many ingenious methods should be seen as having been built upon the foundation of such accumulated wisdom.

The Peculiarity of the Wooden Shutters

The lecture hall's wooden shutters are fitted with rollers to make them easier to open and close. They are also built more sturdily than most such shutters.

The entry for the Shizutani lecture hall contained in *Kokuhō daijiten 5: kenchikubutsu* [Dictionary of National Treasures, vol. 5, Works of Architecture][8] mentions the wooden shutters that run around the four sides of the building. It is unusual for this sort of brief reference work entry to mention something as pedestrian as shutters. Although it simply notes that the wooden shutters are closed every day, the text seems to want to convey what a deep impression the lecture hall makes when they are closed on all sides.

There is a small study on the south side of the lecture hall that served as a place for the feudal lord to stay while visiting and from which he could observe the goings-on in the lecture hall. With a roof lacking tiles, the building has a simplicity reminiscent of a rustic gazebo. While this may seem unusual in a building designed for a lord, this was probably a deliberate choice suggesting an attitude of reserved authority appropriate to an educational site.

As in the lecture hall, the wooden shutters are fitted with rollers but there is no storage case for

---

[7] Okayama Prefectural Board of Education, *Tokubetsu shiseki narabi ni kokuhō oyobi jūyō bunkazai shizutani kō seibyō, shizutani jinja shaden oyobi ishibei hozon shūri (dai niki) kōji hōkokusho* [Report on the Conservation and Repair (Second Phase) of Special Historical Site, National Treasure, and Important Cultural Property Shizutani School Confucian Temple, Shizutani Shrine Main Building, and Stone Walls] (Okayama Prefectural Board of Education, 1962) 42.

[8] Kakichi Suzuki, ed., *Kokuhō daijiten 5: kenchikubutsu* [Dictionary of National Treasures, vol. 5, Works of Architecture] (Kōdansha, 1985) 465.

them on the east side. The shutters on the east face of the small study, then, are rotated 90° at the pillar in the northeast corner and stored in a single shutter case together with the shutters from the north face. Privileging the view from the sitting room led to the adoption of this contrivance of rotating shutters. Enyō-tei, the primary work of architecture at Kōraku-en, was lost to the fires of war but has now been restored. There you can see how the number of pillars was reduced to secure views of the expansive garden and how shutter cases were eliminated as at the Shizutani School's small study.

The Ryūten rest house ^{Fig. 3}, a masterpiece of architecture that also stands in Kōraku-en, boldly inserts a stream through the middle of the open-air space on the building's first level while the upper level offers pleasant views of the expansive garden in all directions. Although the cases for the wooden shutters that cover the long rectangular windows on the sides of the upper level have not been eliminated, they are positioned such that half of their width sticks out from back of the building, a slightly different approach.

Built at the end of the Meiji period, the Gyofūrō guest house at the old Hamaguchi residence (Important Cultural Property, Wakayama prefecture) has tatami matted rooms on three stories to entertain guests. Incredibly, the contrivance here is that after the wooden shutters have been put away in their cases the cases themselves are lowered to the floor below on iron chains. Although this is an extreme example, it is fascinating to consider the various means Japanese have come up with to eliminate pillars and shutter cases that would get in the way of the views seen from Japanese architecture.

At the Shizutani lecture hall, there was no attempt to reduce the number of shutter cases. In other words, no effort was made to change the standard method of positioning one shutter case on each of the building's four faces. There are, however, stairs located at the center of each face other than the west side, and the shutters at these locations are built to accept the addition of small inset doors. Normally, two shutters are provided between each bay. Here, however, since the shutters of the central bays must be provided with inset doors, the width of the shutters was fixed independent of the interval between the outermost pillars. Such points of detail, too, reveal the interesting planning for the building.

The Shōsō-in Repository is perhaps the classic example of monumental Japanese architecture with a door all alone at the center of its façade. Everyone is aware of the importance of the repository, which was used since ancient times as a storehouse to preserve precious relics. The Shizutani lecture hall, on the other hand, is empty inside; nothing that it protects is visible to the eye.

It is a box designed to store the wisdom of philosophy and history over the long term, and a box that gave careful consideration to light. It did not, however, give much thought to the scenery as viewed from inside. It is a box focused first on the light pouring in rather than on wonderful views perceptible to the human eye, and a box carefully designed and constructed to survive the passage of time.

Fig. 3 | Photo by Shigeo Ogawa

Fig. 4 | Shizutani lecture hall with wooden shutters closed.
Photo by Yutaro Tomii

In the evening, the wooden shutters of the lecture hall all rattle shut and the building transforms into something resembling nothing so much as a giant box topped by a roof [Fig.4]. With the sunlight almost completely blocked, the interior becomes a black box. In this way the Shizutani lecture hall—the subject of this volume of photographs—is itself a camera obscura, one with a mirror concealed in the surface of its floor. I note this sense of layeredness in closing as I suspect it is no coincidence.

Acknowledgements

The author wishes to thank Akinori Mizoguchi and Masaki Koiwa for their generous assistance.

References

- Blackman, Aylward M., and T. Eric Peet. "Papyrus Lansing: A Translation with Notes." *Journal of Egyptian Archaeology* 11, no. 3–4 (1925): 284–298.
- Caminos, Ricardo Augusto. *Late-Egyptian Miscellanies*. Brown Egyptological Studies 1, London: Oxford University Press, 1954.
- Fujimori, Terunobu, and Akira Yamaguchi. *Nihon kenchiku shūchū kōgi* [An Intensive Course in Japanese Architecture]. Tankōsha, 2013.
- Fujimori, Terunobu, and Mitsumasa Fujitsuka. *Nihon mokuzō isan: sennen no kenchiku o tabi suru* [Japan's Wooden Heritage: A Journey Through a Thousand Years of Architecture]. Sekai Bunkasha, 2014.
- Hellmann, Marie-Christine. *L'architecture grecque 1: Les principes de la construction* [Greek Architecture, vol.1, Principles of Construction], Paris: Picard, 2002.
- Kobayashi, Toshiko. *Shumeru: jinrui saiko no bunmei* [Sumer: Mankind's Oldest Civilization]. Chūō Kōronsha, 2005.
- Mitsui, Wataru. *Nihon no dentō mokuzō kenchiku: sono kūkan to kōhō* [Japan's Traditional Wooden Architecture: Spaces and Methods of Construction]. Ichigaya Shuppansha, 2016.
- Okayama Prefectural Board of Education, *Tokubetsu shiseki narabi ni kokuhō oyobi jūyō bunkazai shizutani kō kōdō hoka yontō hozon shūri (dai ikki) kōji hōkokusho* [Report on the Conservation and Repair (First Phase) of Special Historical Site, National Treasure, and Important Cultural Property Shizutani School Lecture Hall and Four Outbuildings]. Okayama Prefectural Board of Education, 1961.
- Okayama Prefectural Board of Education, *Tokubetsu shiseki narabi ni kokuhō oyobi jūyō bunkazai shizutani kō seibyō, shizutani jinja shaden oyobi ishibei hozon shūri (dai niki) kōji hōkokusho* [Report on the Conservation and Repair (Second Phase) of Special Historical Site, National Treasure, and Important Cultural Property Shizutani School Confucian Temple, Shizutani Shrine Main Building, and Stone Walls]. Okayama Prefectural Board of Education, 1962.
- Saitō, Yutaka. *Nihon kenchiku no katachi II* [The Essence of Japanese Architecture II]. Toto Shuppan, 2017.
- Sawada, Natari. "Kaoku zakkō" [Notes on Houses]. In *Shintei zōho kojitsu sōsho* 25 [Library of Ancient Customs, Newly Revised and Expanded, vol. 25], edited by Shintei Zōho Kojitsu Sōsho Henshūbu, 221–316. Meiji Tosho Shuppan, 1951 (First edition 1842).
- Sugi, Isamu, et al. *Chikuma sekai bungaku taikei 1: kodai ejiputo shū* [Chikuma World Literature Series, vol. 1, Ancient Egypt]. Chikuma Shobō, 1978.
- Suzuki, Kakichi, ed., *Kokuhō daijiten 5: kenchikubutsu* [Dictionary of National Treasures, vol. 5, Works of Architecture]. Kōdansha, 1985.

小川重雄
—
1958年　　東京都生まれ
1980年　　日本大学藝術学部写真学科卒業後、川澄建築写真事務所入社
1986年　　新建築社入社
1991-2008年 新建築社写真部長
2008年　　小川重雄写真事務所開設
2011年　　岩見沢市にて写真展「Perspective Architecture」
2012年　　東京大学にて写真展「Perspective Architecture」
2014年　　瑞龍寺にて写真展「瑞龍寺――四百年前のモダニズム」
—
現在／2017年：
日本大学藝術学部写真学科非常勤講師、法政大学デザイン工学部建築学科研究科兼任講師、
早稲田大学芸術学校非常勤講師

Shigeo Ogawa
—
1958　　　Born in Tokyo, Japan
1980　　　BFA, Department of Photography, Nihon University College of Art
　　　　　Joined Kawasumi Architectural Photography Office
1986　　　Joined Shinkenchiku-sha Co., Ltd.
1991–2008 Director, Department of Photography, Shinkenchiku-sha Co., Ltd.
2008　　　Established Shigeo Ogawa Studio
2011　　　Solo exhibition *Perspective Architecture* in Iwamizawa City
2012　　　Solo exhibition *Perspective Architecture* at Tokyo University
2014　　　Solo exhibition *Zuiryū-ji Temple: Modernism 400 Years Ago* at Zuiryū-ji Temple
—
Current/2017
Part time lecturer, Department of Photography, Nihon University College of Art
Adjunct lecturer, Hōsei University Graduate School of Engineering & Design
Part-time lecturer, Waseda University Art and Architecture School

西本真一
—
1959年　　東京都生まれ
1987年　　早稲田大学大学院 理工学研究科建設工学専攻博士課程単位取得退学
1994-2007年 早稲田大学理工学部建築学科助教授
2007-2015年 サイバー大学世界遺産学部教授
2015年より 日本工業大学工学部建築学科教授
—
博士（工学）
専門：建築史・保存修復、古代エジプト建築、東南アジア建築技術史
著書：『ファラオの形象――エジプト建築調査ノート（知の蔵書21）』（淡交社、2002）など

Shin'ichi Nishimoto
—
1959　　　Born in Tokyo, Japan
1987　　　Withdrew from the Department of Architecture and Civil Engineering Ph.D. program at the Waseda
　　　　　University Graduate School of Engineering and Science after completing the required credits
1994–2007 Assistant professor, Department of Architecture, Waseda University Faculty of Engineering and Science
2007–2015 Professor, Department of World Heritage, Cyber University
2015　　　Professor, Department of Architecture, Nippon Institute of Technology Faculty of Engineering
—
Ph.D. (Engineering)
Specializations include architectural history, preservation and restoration, the architecture of ancient Egypt, and the history of the architectural technology of Southeast Asia. Publications include *Farao no keishō: ejiputo kenchiku chōsa nōto* [The Shape of the Pharaohs: Research Notes on Egyptian Architecture] (Tankōsha, 2002).

国宝・閑谷学校｜Timeless Landscapes 1

発行日：2017年7月25日 初版第1刷

写真：小川重雄
解説：西本真一
デザイン：秋山伸
図面制作：駒崎継広、半田悠人
翻訳：ハート・ララビー
協力：公益財団法人特別史跡旧閑谷学校顕彰保存会
編集・発行：富井雄太郎

発行所：millegraph
tel & fax：03-5848-9183
mail：info@millegraph.com
http://www.millegraph.com

印刷・製本：図書印刷
佐野正幸／プリンティング・ディレクション
岩瀬学／製本

すべての写真、文章の著作権はそれぞれの写真家および著者に属します。
本書の無断転写、転載、複製は著作権法上の例外を除き禁じられています。

ISBN 978-4-9905436-7-9 C0352
Printed in Japan

Shizutani School (National Treasure)｜Timeless Landscapes 1

Date of publication: 25 July 2017 / First edition, first impression

Photographs: Shigeo Ogawa
Commentary: Shin'ichi Nishimoto
Book design: Shin Akiyama
Diagrams: Tsuguhiro Komazaki, Yuto Handa
English translation: Hart Larrabee
Cooperation: Tokubetsu Shiseki Kyū Shizutani Gakkō Kenshō Hozonkai
Editing and Publication: Yutaro Tomii

Publisher: millegraph
tel & fax: +81-(0)3-5848-9183
info@millegraph.com
http://www.millegraph.com

Printing / Binding: TOSHO Printing Co., Ltd.
Masayuki Sano / Printing Direction
Manabu Iwase / Binding

All photographs and text are copyrighted by their photographer or author.
Unauthorized duplication, reproduction, or copying is prohibited except where permitted under copyright law.

ISBN 978-4-9905436-7-9 C0352
Printed in Japan